Remembering
Jacksonville

Carolyn Williams

TURNER
PUBLISHING COMPANY

From May 29 to October 24, 1898, the Fourth Illinois regiment was stationed here at Camp Cuba Libre, in East Springfield on Ionia Street.

Remembering
Jacksonville

Turner Publishing Company
4507 Charlotte Avenue • Suite 100
Nashville, Tennessee 37209
(615) 255-2665

Remembering Jacksonville

www.turnerpublishing.com

Copyright © 2010 Turner Publishing Company

Library of Congress Control Number: 2010902293

ISBN: 978-1-59652-619-8

Printed in the United States of America

ISBN: 978-1-68336-842-7 (pbk)

CONTENTS

Schooners like the *Lillie* of Key West shown here transported cargo to and from the docks of Jacksonville. Since there were no railroads south of the city, these vessels played an important role in economic development. The St. Johns River was the main artery of trade, providing the only channel of transport for freight and people.

Acknowledgments

This volume, *Remembering Jacksonville,* is the result of the cooperation and efforts of many individuals and organizations. It is with great thanks that we acknowledge in particular the generous assistance of the State Archives of Florida.

We would also like to thank the following individuals for their valuable contributions and assistance in making this work possible:

N. Adam Watson, Photographic Archivist, State Archives of Florida
Carolyn Williams, our writer, Associate Professor of History, University of North Florida in Jacksonville

PREFACE

Jacksonville has thousands of historic photographs that reside in archives, both locally and nationally. This book began with the observation that, while those photographs are of great interest to many, they are not easily accessible. During a time when Jacksonville is looking ahead and evaluating its future course, many people are asking, How do we treat the past? These decisions affect every aspect of the city— architecture, public spaces, commerce, infrastructure—and these, in turn, affect the way that people live their lives. This book seeks to provide easy access to a valuable, objective look into the history of Jacksonville.

The power of photographs is that they are less subjective than words in their treatment of history. Although the photographer can make subjective decisions regarding subject matter and how to capture and present it, photographs seldom interpret the past to the extent textual histories can. For this reason, photography is uniquely positioned to offer an original, untainted look at the past, allowing the viewer to learn for himself what the world was like a century or more ago.

This project represents countless hours of review and research. The researchers have reviewed thousands of photographs in numerous archives. We greatly appreciate the generous assistance of those listed in the acknowledgments of this work, without whom this project could not have been completed.

The goal in publishing this work is to provide broader access to this set of extraordinary photographs which seek to inspire, provide perspective, and evoke insight that might assist people who are responsible for determining Jacksonville's future. In addition, the book seeks to preserve the past with adequate respect and reverence.

With the exception of touching up imperfections that have accrued with the passage of time and cropping where necessary, no changes have been made. The focus and clarity of many images are limited to the technology and the ability of the photographer at the time they were recorded.

The work is divided into eras. Beginning with some of the earliest known photographs of Jacksonville, the first section records photographs from the Civil War to the great fire of 1901. The second section spans the rebirth of the city after the fire to the end of World War I. Section Three moves from the Roaring Twenties to the eve of World War II. The last section covers the war era to the 1960s.

In each of these sections we have made an effort to capture various aspects of life through our selection of photographs. People, commerce, transportation, infrastructure, religious institutions, and educational institutions have been included to provide a broad perspective.

We encourage readers to reflect as they go walking in Jacksonville, strolling through the city, its parks, and its neighborhoods. It is the publisher's hope that in utilizing this work, longtime residents will learn something new and that new residents will gain a perspective on where Jacksonville has been, so that each can contribute to its future.

—Todd Bottorff, Publisher

This building is probably St. Paul's Methodist Church, constructed in 1858 and serving the congregation until 1890, when it was sold to Catholics. The structure was later moved across the street to the corner of Newnan and Duval and used as a hall. It was destroyed by the fire of 1901.

A Long and Slow Beginning
(1860s–1901)

By the time of the war, Jacksonville (incorporated as a city in 1859) was bounded by Hogan's Creek on the north and west Pine Street (today's Main Street) and the St. Johns River on the south. Although much of the fledgling commercial district was destroyed during the four invasions of federal troops, some stores survived the end of the war. This bakery, probably Rivas and Koghman, was located on the north side of Bay Street, between Ocean and Newnan streets.

Union troops built signal towers like the one pictured here to communicate with each other and with ships offshore. This tower was located in what was then called the public square (today Hemming Park). The top of the tower was enclosed to protect the signalmen from Confederate snipers.

After the Battle of Olustee, the most significant Confederate victory in Florida, many of the surviving Union forces retreated to Jacksonville. The federal army continued to occupy the town until federal troops were withdrawn from the state in 1869. During the period of military rule a provost marshal and guard in command handled court cases. The marshal's house stood at the northwest corner of Bay and Ocean streets.

This photo shows Union soldiers gathered at Cooley's commercial establishment.

Members of the Seventy-fifth Ohio Infantry shown here were among the Federal troops in the city until the state surrendered in the spring of 1865.

This U.S. boat house was located at the docks at the foot of Ocean Street.

Samuel B. Hubbard opened one of the first banks in Jacksonville, the Southern Savings and Trust Company, founded in 1888. After the war, his business activities (hardware, house furnishings, and tin, copper, and sheet iron works) were housed in this building downtown at the southeast corner of Main and Forsyth streets. The name was changed to the Mercantile Exchange Bank with S. B. Hubbard, president. This building was destroyed by the fire of 1901.

Until 1895, when its permanent headquarters was constructed at Forsyth and Hogan streets, the location of the post office changed with the postmaster. In the 1880s the post office shared quarters with the custom house at the corner of Bay and Union.

The sawmill and
lumber business,
which characterized
Jacksonville early
on, became a very
lucrative industry in
the period after the
Civil War.

The first mule-drawn trolley cars began operating in Jacksonville in 1880, and the city's first electric streetcar line was introduced 13 years later. Workers like these men laid tracks as the service expanded.

Several banks were established before the Civil War, but none lasted. In 1866, this Freedman's Bank was established for the former slaves in the area. First located at the corner of Bay and Ocean streets, in 1870 the bank operations were moved to this four-story brick building on Forsyth Street. The bank lasted until 1874. This building was destroyed by fire in 1891.

Stanton Institute was established in 1868 by the Freedmen's Bureau and a group of local black citizens to educate African-American children in the area. It was named after Edwin Stanton, who served as President Abraham Lincoln's Secretary of War. The school, pictured here in 1870, provided a grammar school education and was incorporated into the Duval County schools that year.

Among the pupils shown here in front of Stanton Institute in 1880 may have been James Weldon and John Rosamond Johnson. Their mother, Helen Dillet Johnson, taught at the school.

The St. James Hotel was built in 1869, financed by northern capitalists. It grew to be the most famous hotel in the South and was a mecca for wealthy tourists in Florida. The hotel was among the architectural casualties of the Great Fire of 1901. It stood across from Hemming Park.

James Johnson, the father of James Weldon and John Rosamond, served as the head waiter of the St. James Hotel. The wait staff is shown here in the hotel's dining room. It was mainly a winter hotel, catering to guests during that season.

The residence of S. H. Stowe is shown here in 1875.

Riverside, located along the river, in 1869.

A view of
Bull Street.

View of Bay Street, a central business district.

Bay Street from above.

The commercial district eventually expanded onto Main Street, as shown here.

To draw tourists from its chief rival California, city officials decided to hold a "great exposition" of subtropical and tropical products and resources. Entries for the exposition came from all Florida counties, as well as the West Indies and South America. The Subtropical Exposition, held in Springfield, ran from January through May 1888. Among the highlights was a visit by President Grover Cleveland on February 22.

Outdoors at the Subtropical Exposition of 1888.

Before shoe polish there was boot blacking, in Jacksonville as elsewhere.

This group engages in a common leisure activity, picnicking.

Public school developed slowly in the city in the decades following the war. By the 1890s, a number of schools for white and black children had been created in Brooklyn, LaVilla, East Jacksonville, North Jacksonville (Springfield), and Riverside. Horse-drawn school buses like this one transported the children.

On June 13, 1898, Jacksonville was designated the commissary depot of the Seventh Army Signal Corps.

Soldiers at the Signal Corps Camp in 1898.

The whole community was infused with patriotism during the Spanish-American War, as these children demonstrate by staging their own parade.

After the excitement of war receded, community life progressed and recovered stability. The congregation of the Elizabeth Swaim Methodist Church is shown here in 1900.

Street scene around 1900.

Jacksonville, like the rest of the post–Civil War South, was a predominantly Democratic city. On June 19-22, 1900, the last Democratic state convention was held in the city.

The city went up in smoke on May 3, 1901. The fire consumed 2,000 buildings and took the lives of 7 people. This view shows the New South city that Jacksonville had become by 1909, less than a decade after the Great Fire. The city's first "skyscraper," at left, the new 10-story Bisbee Building designed by Henry Klutho, was the first reinforced-concrete frame high-rise building in the state of Florida.

IMPORTANT NEW SOUTH CITY
(1902–1919)

The old Duval County Courthouse, shown here in 1912, was completed the year after the fire. Two years later it would be expanded by an annex. The courthouse building was demolished in 1960.

The city built its first major library building after the fire with the assistance of steel magnate Andrew Carnegie, who offered $50,000 if the city would provide a site and agree to allocate an annual $5,000 to the building's maintenance. The result, at the northeast corner of Ocean and Adams streets, is shown here. The library opened to the public in 1905.

Forsyth Street became the heart of Jacksonville's banking industry, and Jacksonville was the banking center of the state in the early 1900s. Here is a view of Forsyth Street looking north (named after General John Forsyth, U.S. Minister to Spain, who helped conduct the negotiations for the acquisition of Florida).

The Florida National Bank shown here next to the Bisbee Building in 1910 began in 1902 as the Mercantile Exchange Bank. Later it was purchased by the Florida Bank and Trust and became part of the Florida National Bank chain.

Forsyth Street looking north in 1912.

This scene of Bay Street looking north from Laura Street reveals a glimpse of Furchgotts Department Store. Also visible are the various modes of transportation—the trolley, bicycles, the ubiquitous horse-driven wagon, and automobiles, which were rapidly multiplying on the streets of Jacksonville.

This view of West Bay Street looking southward provides a close-up of the trolleys and the Greenleaf and Crosby Clock at the northwest corner of Laura and Adams streets.

The Windsor Hotel (pictured here in 1903) began as a three-story wooden structure occupying the lot at the northwest corner of Hogan and Monroe streets in 1875. Shown here in 1902, the Windsor was the only large hotel destroyed by the 1901 fire and rebuilt. The new building was made of brick, stone, and steel, divided into sections by fire walls, and had accommodations for 500 guests.

The Duval Hotel, shown here in 1908, opened in 1893 at the northwest corner of Hogan and Forsyth streets and was one of the few buildings to survive the Great Fire. It partly rests on the most historic spot in Jacksonville—the site of the first house built in the city.

By the second decade of the twentieth century, automobiles were not only a means of transportation but also for some a hobby. The three men posing here in 1915 appear to be changing a flat.

People shown here are fishing off one of the city's piers in the early 1900s, a traditional leisure activity in Jacksonville.

Children employed at various jobs, like these Western Union messenger boys, were also a common sight. When this picture was taken in 1913, the Western Union Telegraph Company was located at Bay and Laura streets.

The *Florida Times-Union,* originally the *Florida Union* in 1864, later became the *Florida Times-Union and Citizen.* In 1903, the paper adopted its current name. These young men are employed in the advertising department of the newspaper.

Florida Times-Union employees doing linotype in 1911.

Women soon became the telephone operators, but here men are seen testing a telephone switchboard in 1914. According to early Jacksonville historian T. Frederick Davis, the first telephone in operation in Jacksonville (and perhaps Florida) was a "private line connecting the office of A. M. Beck at Bay and Pine (Main) streets with Inland Navigation Company at the foot of Laura Street."

The city government first authorized funds for a fire department in 1886. Fire Department No. 2 was first located at the west side of Main Street between Church and Ashley streets. In 1898, it was moved to the west side of Main Street between State and Orange. After the fire the station was rebuilt on the same site, and by 1915, when this photograph of firemen and their horse-driven wagon was taken, the department was stationed on the southeast corner of 4th and Main streets in Springfield.

African-American men were chief among the workers along the city's docks. This 1912 picture shows dockworkers at their dinner (lunch) hour.

Because of the yellow fever and other epidemics in the nineteenth century, the city had learned the value of providing residents with an adequate water supply. These men are laying water pipes. Also visible is the Palms Hotel.

An employee in the Water Department's meter shop in 1914.

This festive scene is a view of Forsyth Street in 1914. The flags of both the U.S. and the Confederacy are shown proudly waving.

In this view of Forsyth Street, at the intersection of Hogan, the Windsor Hotel is visible at left.

This view of Forsyth Street at the intersection of Hogan Street reveals movie theaters, which were becoming part of the cityscape. The Metropolis and Imperial theaters are partly visible at opposite sides.

The shipbuilding industry that began in Jacksonville in the 1800s was given a boost by the Great War. Besides constructing new vessels for the war, local shippers benefited from the ongoing repair work. Ships awaiting repair are shown here in 1918.

Ship repairs under way in 1918.

As early as 1907, the Florida legislature authorized the establishment of a permanent state military camp. The camp was completed in 1909 to be used as a Florida National Guard base. Later it was taken over and expanded by the federal government and reopened in 1917 as camp James E. Johnston (for the Confederate general who before the Civil War was quartermaster of the U.S. Army). After World War I the camp was renamed J. Clifford Foster.

World War I–era soldiers at Camp Johnston.

Camp Johnston soldiers at an outdoor mess.

ROARING TWENTIES TO GREAT DEPRESSION
(1920–1939)

The expansion of the business district to Adams Street is shown here. Automobiles have replaced horse-driven wagons and trolleys as the vehicle of choice.

This good will tour of Jacksonville businessmen before the Great Depression illustrates that times were good and expectations of greater prosperity high.

The Atlantic Coast Line Railroad owned this building, which housed a number of other businesses.

A Union Station side street.

People arrive at and depart Union Station by car and trolley, as the numbers of automobiles in the station parking lot climb.

To accommodate the growing railroad lines, the city built its first main bridge across the St. Johns River. Before the bridge, railway cars were ferried on barges.

Car races had become the rage by the jazz age. This photograph shows celebrity race-car driver Sig Haughdahl in his Fiat with his personal mechanic Jimmy Chai in 1921. In the early 1900s automobile races began at Atlantic Beach.

Line-up for an auto race at the Jacksonville Fairgrounds in 1922.

While Henry Ford's cars were being marketed to the common man, a demand for luxury cars rose. Here mechanics and other employees, likely of the Claude Nolan Cadillac Company, pose for a group shot. This company was founded in 1907 and is the oldest car dealership in the city.

The greatest celebrity of the 1920s, the Lone Eagle Charles Lindbergh is shown here with his *Spirit of St. Louis* on a stop in Jacksonville during the nationwide tour following his famous transatlantic flight.

These young women seem not to have a care in the world as they pose for the camera on the wings of an airplane on the beach. By this time airplanes were no longer a novelty. Many people had seen the stunts of barnstorming pilots, and some had flown.

Members of the Woodmen of the World Life Insurance Society pose at Mayport in 1930. Little of the Depression that began the preceding year is in evidence.

Officers of the U.S. Army, Lieutenant Colonel J. H. Spengler and Major Fred H. Davis are shown at Camp J. Clifford R. Foster (former Camp Johnston). Major Davis served as the state attorney general from 1927 to 1931.

The Duval Motor Company on West Forsyth Street near Lee Street, one of the city's automobile dealerships, is shown here in 1930. Despite the hard times, Jacksonville business faced forward, confident of renewed prosperity.

These men are beneficiaries of the New Deal programs initiated through tax dollars by President Roosevelt. As enlistees in the Federal Emergency Relief Administration, they are employed here laying track for airport construction.

The Mason Hotel, 11 stories tall, was constructed of steel, granite, and brick. Built for George M. Mason for $1 million, the hotel opened to the public in 1913 with 250 guest rooms. Located on Bay Street, it afforded a view of the St. Johns River from penthouse apartments and became one of Jacksonville's most popular hotels. It was later called the Mayflower.

A Smith, Richardson & Conroy delivery truck in 1933.

Men with safety inspection vehicles stand in front of the L. S. Teague auto repair shop in 1936.

The Arcade Theatre on Adams Street was another popular movie house in the 1930s. The French Novelty and Modern Luggage shops, which added to downtown commerce, are also visible.

The commercial establishments shown here in 1939 include the Lane Drugstore and the Rainbow Grill on Forsyth Street.

Women employees at a crab-processing plant remove meat from the shells in 1939.

Founded in 1875 as the first secondary school for whites in Jacksonville, Duval High School is shown here in 1936. The original school building was constructed in 1877 and used until destroyed in the Great Fire of 1901. After assuming temporary quarters in the LaVilla Grammar School, the school moved to the new building completed in 1908. This building was used until the 1970s, when it was converted into an apartment complex called Duval-Stevens Apartments.

Shown here in 1937, the Roosevelt Hotel, formerly the Carling Hotel, was built in the mid-1920s on West Adams Street. When it opened in 1926 it was advertised as having the "latest equipment in the rooms." After being vacant for a number of years, the building was renovated into condominiums.

A Baptist Church formed in Jacksonville in 1838. This structure, built after the Great Fire, is shown here at the corner of Hogan and Church streets in 1935.

The Riverside Presbyterian church building, pictured here in 1939, was built in 1927. The original building, known as the "Little Brown Church," was demolished on this site in 1925.

Boy Scouts in a circus parade in downtown Jacksonville in 1939.

Automobiles on the beaches of Florida became a commonplace part of the landscape. Shown here is a day at the beach in 1936.

People on the beach in the 1930s.

A Ferris wheel and other carnival rides at the beach in the 1930s.

People fishing from the pier in the 1930s.

Amusement and shopping at the beach in the 1930s.

This view of Adams Street in 1938 suggests a dreary Depression-era day. On the national scene by this time, a partial recovery was under way.

The growth of major department stores in the twenties is illustrated by the Levy Building shown here. This structure, located on West Adams Street, was built in 1927.

President Roosevelt inspects personnel at the new Naval Air Station in the 1940s.

FROM WORLD WAR II TO RECENT TIMES
(1940–1960s)

On the eve of U.S. entry to the war, life was calm and normal in the city. The economy seemed to be recovering. This view of Forsyth Street in 1940 shows the new stores Thom McAn, Butler's Shoes, F. W. Woolworth, as well as the Arcade Theatre and the Florida National Bank.

Here men prepare ribs for the Main Street Bridge barbecue.

By the twentieth century, bridges connected the parts of the city separated by the St. Johns River. Here the new Main Street Bridge opens in 1941.

The J. C. Penney Store on Hogan Street is shown here. This store, as well as Sears and Woolworth, would be targets of civil rights activists in 1960.

Many young men were trained as pilots, including the brother of future president John F. Kennedy, Joseph P. Kennedy, Jr., at the Naval Air Station in Jacksonville. This photo shows an instructor and students of the VN-11A primary training squadron (ca. 1941).

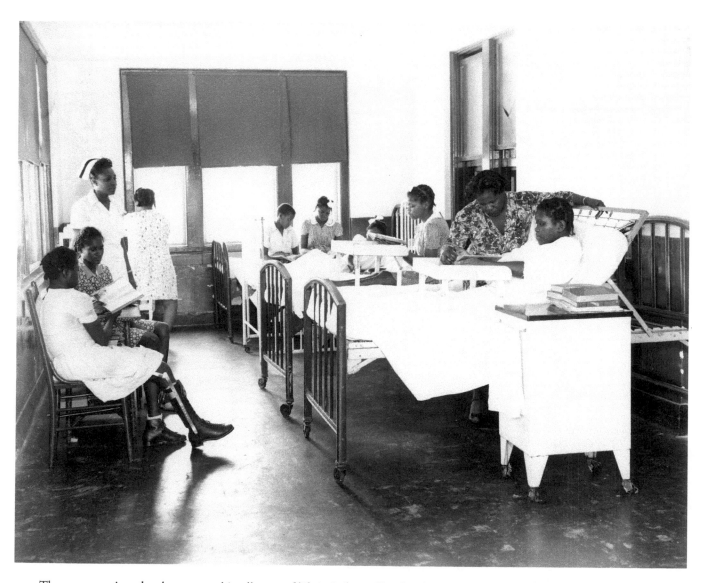

The races continued to be separated in all areas of life in Jacksonville after the war. This is a photograph of Brewster Hospital's children's ward. Brewster Hospital, located on Jefferson Street, was created for African-Americans in the early twentieth century when only the county hospital accepted black patients. In the 1980s and 1990s, it served as hospice space for Memorial Hospital. The building was demolished in 2006.

First Presbyterian
Church in 1946.

As this photo of Adams Street shows, the city, particularly streets near the river and other bodies of water, continued to be plagued by flooding.

In the postwar era the railroads continued to be an important part of the Jacksonville economy. These men shown here in 1945 are machinists for the Seaboard Air Line Railway Company.

Smaller businesses continued to proliferate in the postwar years. Here two men stand beside a truck in front of the Grosse and Millican Electric Company.

This soldier has apparently won the car parked behind him from Dollar Motors, a used-car dealership.

The Kress five-and-dime was a leading example of discount stores, which grew in number in the postwar years.

Automobiles continued to proliferate around the city. Shown here are men on the floor of the showroom at the Duval Motor Company in 1948.

The docks continued to be an important aspect of the urban landscape. This is a view of Jacksonville dockside, in 1946.

The service attendant became a staple during the 1940s. An attendant is shown here at the airport service station in 1949.

Ford Motor Company employees in training in 1949.

Automobile traffic crosses the Main Street Bridge here in 1949.

Trucks and employees of the Gate City Mattress and Carpet Works, shown here in 1949.

Women employees of Fram Florida can-storage plant, on Stockton Street, shown here in 1949.

This photo shows the Schlitz Beer neon sign used to attract customers.

Eating out became possible for more people. Family restaurants like Biser's were becoming common in the late 1940s and 1950s.

This street scene shows the thriving business district downtown in 1950.

The city's business district on Laura Street in 1949.

A crowd watches television in a store window in 1954.

The suburban shopping center of Five Points is highlighted here in this street sign decorated at the intersection.

An Eastern Air Lines plane at Jacksonville Airport, 1956.

Most people continued to travel by train. The Atlantic Coast Line train is shown here in 1960.

This 1960s aerial view reveals the city's progress.

The number of marinas on the St. Johns River grew as river vessels multiplied. Here the *Corky II* rests at Sims Brothers Marina in 1960.

The Gator Bowl served as a municipal stadium for the city beginning in the 1930s. One of the most famous events is the college football rival game, the Florida-Georgia classic. This is an aerial view of the Gator Bowl in 1961.

More schools were built during this period. Assembled here is a graduating class at Southside Grammar School on Flagler Avenue.

Crowds gather at Hemming Park to listen to Lyndon Johnson speak.

Notes on the Photographs

These notes, listed by page number, attempt to include all aspects known of the photographs. Each of the photographs is identified by the page number, a title or description, photographer and collection, archive, and call or box number when applicable. Although every attempt was made to collect all data, in some cases complete data may have been unavailable due to the age and condition of some of the photographs and records.

70 **RACE-CAR DRIVER SIG HAUDAHL WITH MECHANIC JIMMIE CHAI**
State Archives of Florida
RC10425

71 **LINE-UP AT THE JACKSONVILLE FAIRGROUNDS**
State Archives of Florida
N041975

72 **MEN POSED IN CADILLAC GARAGE**
State Archives of Florida
N032611

73 **CHARLES LINDBERGH WITH THE SPIRIT OF ST. LOUIS**
State Archives of Florida
N027973

74 **YOUNG WOMEN POSING ON AN AIRPLANE PARKED ON THE BEACH**
State Archives of Florida
SP01276

75 **FIRST ANNUAL WOODMEN OF THE WORLD FAIR**
State Archives of Florida
N034836

76 **LT. COL. J. H. SPENGLER AND MAJOR FRED H. DAVIS**
State Archives of Florida
N028585

77 **DUVAL MOTOR COMPANY**
State Archives of Florida
SP01913

78 **LAYING RAILROAD TRACK FOR AIRPORT CONSTRUCTION**
State Archives of Florida
N032903

79 **FLORIDA THEATRE AND STAFF**
State Archives of Florida
N033201

80 **HOTEL MASON ON A BUSY STREET**
State Archives of Florida
SP00281

81 **DELIVERY TRUCK**
State Archives of Florida
SP02440

82 **TRUCK AND CAR IN FRONT OF AN AUTO REPAIR SHOP**
State Archives of Florida
SP02435

83 **ARCADE THEATRE**
State Archives of Florida
SP01936

84 **STREET SCENE**
State Archives of Florida
SP02717

85 **CRAB PLANT, WITH WOMEN REMOVING MEAT FROM SHELLS**
State Archives of Florida
SP00436

86 **DUVAL COUNTY HIGH SCHOOL**
State Archives of Florida
SP01580

87 **ROOSEVELT HOTEL**
State Archives of Florida
SP00396

88 **BAPTIST CHURCH BUILDING ON THE CORNER OF HOGAN AND CHURCH**
State Archives of Florida
SP00699

89 **RIVERSIDE PRESBYTERIAN CHURCH**
State Archives of Florida
SP00697

90 **BOY SCOUTS IN THE CIRCUS PARADE**
State Archives of Florida
SP02894

91 **CARS ON THE BEACH**
State Archives of Florida
SP02700

92 **PEOPLE ON THE BEACH**
State Archives of Florida
SP02692

93 **FERRIS WHEEL AND RIDES**
State Archives of Florida
SP02688

94 **PEOPLE FISHING FROM PIER**
State Archives of Florida
SP02684

95 **AMUSEMENT AND SHOPPING AT THE BEACH**
State Archives of Florida
SP02694

96 **STREET SCENE**
State Archives of Florida
N033091

97 **LEVY BUILDING**
State Archives of Florida
SP01921

98 **ROOSEVELT INSPECTING NAVAL AIR STATION PERSONNEL**
State Archives of Florida
PR20036

100 **STREET SCENE**
State Archives of Florida
SP02747

101 **MEN BARBECUING RIBS**
State Archives of Florida
C017866

102 **BRIDGE OPENING**
State Archives of Florida
SP02730

103 **J. C. PENNEY COMPANY**
State Archives of Florida
SP00395

104 **INSTRUCTOR AND STUDENTS OF PRIMARY TRAINING SQUADRON**
State Archives of Florida
PR20035

105 **BREWSTER HOSPITAL'S CHILDREN'S WARD**
State Archives of Florida
SP00950

106 **FIRST PRESBYTERIAN**
State Archives of Florida
SP00680

107 **ADAMS STREET AFTER HEAVY RAINS FLOOD JACKSONVILLE**
State Archives of Florida
C005715

108 **MACHINISTS FOR THE SEABOARD AIR LINE RAILWAY COMPANY**
State Archives of Florida
SP01309

109 **TRUCK IN FRONT OF ELECTRIC COMPANY**
State Archives of Florida
SP02314

110 **DOLLAR MOTORS PRESENTING A MAN WITH A CAR**
State Archives of Florida
SP00214

Printed in the USA
CPSIA information can be obtained
at www.ICGtesting.com
JSHW072021140824
68134JS00042B/3734